What It's All About!

Reclaiming Christianity's Essence: Christ In Me

Joel Backstrom
B.A., M.Div., M.Ed.

XULON PRESS

I dedicate this book to my three sons,

Benjamin, Zachariah, and Thomas,

and to the memory of my father,

Charles W. Backstrom

CONTENTS

Introduction

I pray that out of His glorious riches He may
strengthen you with power through His Spirit
in your inner being, so that Christ may dwell in
your hearts through faith. And I pray that you,
being rooted and established in love, may have
power, together with all the saints, to grasp how
wide and long and high and deep is the love
of Christ, and to know this love that surpasses
knowledge – that you may be filled to the mea-
sure of all the fullness of God
Ephesians 3: 16-19

There is a drought silently creeping over the landscape of American Christianity these days. Corporately it is sapping the energy of the Christian church and weakening its influence in our culture. Individually it dries out the soul of a believer leaving behind a vague hollowness, a lack of joy, and, in all likelihood, an unstated sense of disappointment with one's faith.

No, it is not a matter of unconfessed or persistent sin, although each and every one of us who claims to be a Christian will always continue to struggle with sin and the consequent robbery of joy that comes with it. Rather, it is a matter of misplaced emphasis that all too often affects even the most sanctified, mature, and devoted of Christians. Sadly, this joy-robbing emphasis is very much engrained in the very culture of the American church. Many who have been Christians all their lives will be the first to confess that they, too, have experienced the dull, dry hollowness that results when one's life is affected by this malady. Most of you who read this have experienced it as well, although you may never have identified it in any specific terms.

The purpose for the writing of this book is to bring this misplaced emphasis to light and to, hopefully, be of help in causing us to remain constantly vigilant lest we fall victim to its drying influence once again. The joy we all seek to enjoy on a more consistent basis is available to us. It is God's intent that we experience it as we return to the very essence of our Christianity, that being the mystery, the phenomenon, if you will, of "Christ in me". May God add his blessing to the intent of the words which follow.

Chapter One

Let Your Light So Shine...

You are the salt of the earth. But if the salt loses
its saltiness, how can it be made salty again?
It is no longer good for anything, except to be
thrown out and trampled by men. You are the
light of the world. A city on a hill can not be
hidden. Neither do people light a lamp and put
it under a bowl. Instead they put it on its stand,
and it gives light to everyone in the house. In
the same way, let your light shine before men,
that they may see your good deeds and praise
your Father in heaven.
Matthew 5:13-16

I n Matthew 5:16 we read: "Let your light so shine among men, that they may see your good works and glorify your Father in heaven". For most of my life, I thought of my "light" as being my good deeds, and the driving force behind much of the outlook and out-working of my Christianity was the compulsion to try to let my light shine, to show the depth of my Christianity, through the works I engaged in.

I was not alone in this pursuit. Virtually every Christian I knew as a young man growing up in the church modeled this form of thinking. The perception that I caught from the evangelical culture around me was that, once you'd come to know Christ personally, your "new life" consisted in actively engaging in a certain lifestyle and doing certain things. A partial recitation of those things involved in this lifestyle would include such things as: (a) subscribing to a sort of "list Christianity" for individual believers that mandated a fairly specific behavior code of do's and don't's; (b) witnessing to the "lost" using one of the many cookbook methods currently available, whether they were open to it or not; and, (c) being actively involved in the visible ministries of the local church to the exclusion of almost all other outside activities.

The exact details of the expected lifestyle may have differed somewhat from group to group, but Christians I knew all seemed to be caught up in this same basic approach to their Christianity.

From my perspective as a young Christian, this brand of Christianity kept people so on edge that they couldn't possibly have had time to actually find joy in their relationship with Christ, much less come to an internal understanding of what "Christ in me" really means or what simply "being" a Christ-follower was all about. I went through a time of searching and questioning over this, but, unfortunately, over time I simply grew hardened to the apparent contradiction between "joy in the Lord" and "letting your light shine". Eventually I came to accept that this is just the way it is; that people talk about the joy of the Lord but that there is really no such thing, at least not on an ongoing basis. It is just something that is part of your vocabulary as a Christian but there is no real substance behind the words.

In retrospect I believe that my transition to a joyless brand of Christianity was typical for the average evangelical Christian, then and now. It goes something like this. A person is introduced to Christ and urged to receive Him as Lord and Savior and to come to know Him personally through an ongoing study of the Bible and Bible-based literature. This is, of course, entirely biblical and very well done in most evangelical and conservative churches in the country. However, once this "knowing" component comes to life in the believer, there seems to be a rush to move that individual into actively "doing" Christianity, and to let their light shine via that doing, without allowing the soul adequate time to feed on the truths of the faith and the personal implications of those truths for them, their attitudes, and their spiritual dispositions.

The rush to prescribe an evangelically acceptable, activistic Christianity to impressionable and vulnerable souls, as well as the unstated implication that this is really the essence of true, mature Christianity, can and will do irreparable damage to these individuals, a tragedy that is all too real in the lives of countless, joy-deprived Christians across the face of this country, if not the entire world.

So what does it mean to "let your light so shine"? What is the essence of Christianity if it does not consist in a life of actively doing "kingdom work", as we so often hear? How can we get to the point where our light so shines that people really will see our good works and recognize that this truly must be a "God-thing" that they are witnessing in our lives? In the rest of this book we will look more closely into these matters and hopefully arrive at satisfactory, biblical answers.

Chapter Two

Internalized Christ, Not Externalized Christianity

Through the law I died to the law so that I might
live for God. I have been crucified with Christ
and I no longer live, but Christ lives in me. The
life I live in the body, I live by faith in the Son of
God, who loved me and gave himself for me...
My dear children, for whom I am again in the
pains of childbirth until Christ is formed in you,
how I wish I could be with you now and change
my tone, because I am perplexed about you...
It is for freedom that Christ has set us free. Stand
firm, then, and do not let yourselves be bur-
dened by a yoke of slavery.
Galatians 2:19-20; 4:19-20; 5:1

In Colossians 1:27, the apostle Paul says that God has
chosen to make known among the Gentiles the glorious riches of a mystery, "which is Christ in you, the hope

of glory". What in the world does he mean? I think it is safe to state, on the basis of the wider context of Scripture, that he means exactly what he says, that the mystery of New Testament Christianity is the phenomenon of Christ literally living in the life of the believer. Not only is He with us (Matthew 28:20 et al), He is also in us and that introduces a whole new aspect of what it means to be a Christian.

We are not talking here about the process of receiving Christ and the gracious act of justification whereby we are seen by God the Father as being "in Christ" and clothed in His "robes of righteousness". The New Testament epistles are rife with wonderful passages that relate to the benefits and privileges of being "in Christ", especially those epistles written by Paul, Peter, and John. The assumption being made of you, the reader, is that this process has already happened in you, you are already in Christ, and that you are now inquiring regarding what it truly means to "be" a Christian - to have Christ in you, and to let your light so shine that others may see your good deeds and recognize God at work in you.

In the Matthew 5:16 passage, it is noteworthy that Jesus says, "let your light shine before men SO THAT they may see your good deeds and glorify your Father in heaven". It is evident from that statement that the light precedes the good deeds. The light is not the good deeds themselves. The light comes into existence before the good deeds do, making them remarkable only because of the light that shines in and through them.

Anyone can do good deeds. That ability in and of itself is totally unremarkable. Even the pagans do good deeds for others, as Christ Himself pointed out (Matthew 5:46-47). What then is this light that makes the good deeds of the Christian stand out? It is, in fact, the phenomenon of Christ in me – the mystery of which the apostle Paul spoke. It precedes the good deeds and is, in fact, a state of being, a state of existence unique to the born-again Christian soul. It is included as part of the package of being saved through faith, and is not of ourselves, but is a gift of God (Ephesians 2:8) and it is at work in you right now if you have truly been saved by faith in Christ alone.

When I was in seminary in the late 1980's, one of my professors introduced us to a philosophy of Christian living that I will call the "Know – Be – Do" philosophy. I latched onto it then but did not really grasp it at the heart level or put it into place in my life until much later. The "Know – Be –Do" way of living the Christian life specifies three distinct aspects of Christian living. The second of these aspects, the "Be" aspect strikes very near to the heart of what "Christ in me" Christianity is all about.

First, in the "Know" aspect, one comes to know Jesus personally and learns more about Him via hearing and studying the Bible. Then, in the "Be" aspect, one incorporates what it means to actually be a Christian into one's own thinking, attitudes, and lifestyle. In other words, one internalizes what "Christ in me" really means and allows that to mold one's character. Finally, one launches forth from that sense of being and of "Christ in me" into the works which God calls them to do in the natural course of progressing through a life whose operating principle is the constant awareness of the supernatural fact of Christ in me.

When this is the case, the emphasis of the Christian life changes from the predominant view of our Christian culture that it is all about me living for Christ to the view that it is really about Christ living in and through me. This is a very important and liberating distinction. The apostle Paul makes this exact point when he says in Galatians 2:20: "I have been crucified with Christ and I no longer live, but Christ lives in me". He is indeed talking about the "Christ in me" phenomenon - from which the whole of one's Christianity and good deeds flow - when all is as it should be.

There are so many tragic stories about people who have never gotten this straight and have suffered need-lessly on account of it. Many have obsessed all their lives over having missed out on God's best for their lives on account of the unbiblical idea that the quality of their relationship with God is based on what they have done or not done. A Christian woman in my church circle went to her grave an unhappy person because she believed she had not fulfilled God's will for her life because she never made it to the mission field. Even my own father, a godly and grace-filled man, was afflicted by this at times in his later years and lamented out loud occasionally that he had "not done enough" for God. Those of us who really knew him knew better than to listen to this; we all loved and cherished him for simply being the wonderful person that Christ living in him empowered him to be. The point being made is that it is probably inevitable in our performance-valuing society that we will all fall victim to this snare of the devil at times, but having the proper perspective will enable us to minimize the damage it does in us.

In my own life, as I mentioned earlier, I'd heard about the "Know – Be – Do" perspective in seminary, but it really didn't take hold in me until I was in my middle forties. Being an academician of sorts, I had always tended to intellectualize my Christianity and thus emphasized the "know" aspects of Christianity in my family life, my church life, and my personal life.

Then at forty-four years of age I finally realized a long-time aspiration and was accepted into the U.S. Army as a chaplain in the Reserve and National Guard. Here a transformation of my thinking began to occur. Both in chaplaincy training at Fort Jackson, SC, as well as in serving my unit back in North Dakota, I soon learned that, contrary to my expectations, the most effective Army chaplains were those who learned the art of MBWA – that is "ministry by walking around".

Soldiers, by enlarged, are not going to be impacted by the wonderful worship services or counseling opportunities the chaplain provides, but they are going to remember him and seek him out if he simply enters into their niches and lets them get to know him for who he is and see that he truly is a "man of the cloth" who not only wears the cross on his lapel but allows the light of that cross to shine through him into any situation encountered. They are not necessarily going to remember him for what he did, but they will remember him for who he was.

I learned that lesson then, and soon recognized that the same is true when it comes to what we often call our "legacy". We obsess over doing the right things so that we will be remembered the way we want to be remembered, but the truth is that we will be remembered by those who know us, not for the things we do, but for who we are – not for our "doing", but for our "being". I think you'll agree that this always has been and will continue to be the case both in family life and in church life.

"Being" a Christian person who is memorable for the right reasons is a product of "Christ in me" and the degree to which that mystery is allowed to work itself out in our lives. Those individuals who we would all agree on as being "great Christians" became great, not by concentrating on doing great things, but by being content with being what the Christ in them led them to be. They became great, not by obsessing about being great and leaving a great legacy, but by allowing Christ to be formed in them (Galatians 4:19), whatever that meant in their particular case, usually without a second thought to self or how what they were doing looked to others. They did not see themselves as self-sacrificing; they loved "being" what they were called to be and would not have had it any other way.

The New Testament typically does not focus in too closely on specific things that we are to do; but it does pointedly emphasize what we are to be. The fruits of the Spirit for example, (and we will talk much more about the Spirit in the next chapter), are not a to-do list; they are a to-be list. We are not called to do things that make us appear to be loving, joyful, peaceable, patient, kind, good, faithful, gentle, and self-controlled. We are called to BE loving, joyful, peaceable, patient, kind, good, faithful, gentle, and self-controlled. Elsewhere, we are often called on to BE humble, compassionate, and the like - not to DO specific acts that give the impression that we are those things. Yet that is the constant pressure we face as Christians in our Christian circles. Appearances are valued and carefully groomed; sadly, what you really are when no one else sees is given short shrift.

It is so important to realize that, no matter how many good deeds a person may do, a convincing light will never shine forth from that life until the fact is accepted that externalized Christianity is a dead end road. Ultimately it will not bring you fulfillment and the bare facts are that God is not nearly as interested in what you do as He is in who you are, and in the extent to which His Son lives in you.

Chapter Three

Into My Heart, Come Into My Heart, Lord Jesus

Those whom I love I rebuke and discipline. So
be earnest, and repent. Here I am! I stand at the
door and knock. If anyone hears my voice and
opens the door, I will come in and eat with him,
and he with me. To him who overcomes, I will
give the right to sit with me on my throne, just
as I overcame and sat down with my Father on
his throne. He who has an ear, let him hear what
the Spirit says to the churches
Revelation 3:19-22

I f it is true that a vital Christian life is more a matter of
being than it is of doing, such that the being actually
leads to more effective doing – and if it is also true that
being what we are intended to be comes about as Christ

enters more and more deeply into our lives, the question then becomes: What must happen for this to take place?

When we were little kids in Sunday School, we used to sing a little ditty that went:

Into my heart, into my heart,

Come into my heart, Lord Jesus.

Come in today, come in to stay,

Come into my heart Lord Jesus.

I believe that little song has it right. That is what it's all about. Having Christ continually coming into one's life and making Himself known in and through that life is what it's all about for a Christian.

In Revelation 3:20 Jesus says: "Here I am. I stand at the door and knock. If anyone hears my voice and opens the door, I will come in and eat with him and he with Me". That verse is often used for evangelistic purposes to show that Christ desires to be in relationship with us. I'll not question the appropriateness of doing so; but it is not contextually correct. This verse in context is clearly written to converted church members who now stand in need of self-examination and repentance, and Jesus is asking them to allow Him to have access into the deeper recesses of their hearts and lives.

Other Scriptures also sound the same theme albeit with different methods of expression. Hebrews 12:2 urges us to "fix our eyes on Jesus, the author and perfecter of our faith". Colossians 3:1 reminds us: "Since, then, you have been raised with Christ, set your hearts on things above, where Christ is seated at the right hand of God". Several other references with similar inferences could also be quoted at this point.

So how do we "open the door"? How do we "fix our eyes on Jesus" or "set our hearts on things above"? Is it simply a matter of us having to bear down, discipline ourselves, and focus? Or is it more than that?

Oh, it is so much more than that. And praise God that is is. For this is where the Holy Spirit enters the picture. This is His territory. The New Testament is full of references that verify that the work of the Holy Spirit within us is to remind us of Christ, to help us focus on Him, and to bring the very life of Christ to reality within us. Radio Bible teacher Charles Stanley put it aptly and succinctly in a March 2011 radio message: "The Holy Spirit releases the life of Christ within us".[1]

In John 14:13, Jesus Himself says: "But the Counselor, the Holy Spirit, whom the Father will send in my name, will teach you all things and will remind you of everything I have said to you". In John 15:26, He says: "When the Counselor comes, whom I will send to you from the Father, the Spirit of truth who goes out from the Father, He will testify about me". And in John 16:13-14, He adds: "But when He, the Spirit of truth comes, He will guide you into all truth. He will not speak on His own; He will speak only what He hears, and He will tell you what is yet to come. He will bring glory to Me by taking from what is Mine and making it known to you".

The Holy Spirit is referred to as a counselor, a guide, and a helper. These roles all point to the fact that, at least for now, His role is to point us to Jesus, to remind us of Jesus, and to enable the life of Christ, that Christ in me phenomenon, to become reality within me and form the very core of my being from which all else flows. The Apostle Paul in Ephesians 3:16-17 puts it this way: "I pray that out his glorious riches he may strengthen you with power through his Spirit in your inner being, so that Christ may dwell in your hearts through faith".

The Holy Spirit will take the lion's share of the responsibility for bringing out in us the life of Christ, and in the process enabling us to simply be what we are intended to be. But we do play a role in this. The Holy Spirit will make it all happen within us, for we cannot do this ourselves, but we must choose to cooperate with Him or all His work will be stifled and never come to fruition. In other words, we have the option to stop the work of the

Holy Spirit if we do not follow His urging, His counsel, His guiding, and His desire to help us.

What are the things he will urge us to do in order to cooperate with Him in this work of bringing the life of Christ to reality within us? There is no great mystery here. The many Spirit-provided "tools", or means of help, made available to help us toward that gracious and wonderful result are well documented in the Bible. First and foremost, we are to read the Word of God through which God supernaturally speaks to us; we are to reflect and meditate upon that Word, and we are to respond to the God of the Bible via a faithful prayer life. Those are basics we are all quite familiar with, I'm sure.

But there are many other useful "tools" or means of help available to us as well. Let me list just a few: 1) We can very intentionally ask the Holy Spirit to provide us with enlightenment and direction. 2) We can take the time to recount and praise our Lord for the blessings we have already experienced. 3) We can spend time in the company of other Christians participating with them in things that are "spiritually discerned". 4) We can live a life characterized by self-examination and confession, recrucifying daily the old nature that still wields its power so often in our lives. The Holy Spirit will work within us individually in these and other ways, always prompting us to employ those tools most suited to our personalities and circumstances.

Incidentally, for those Christians who come under the umbrella of "sacramental Christianity" there is an additional, very powerful, tool available. These Christians hold to the faith-strengthening belief that, in the sacrament of the Lord's Supper, Jesus Christ literally gives to believers His very self via His "Real Presence" in the elements. Thus, for these Christians, every celebration of the Lord's Supper is a vivid and palpable reminder of the reality of "Christ in me". Of course, all Christians who believe in the atoning work of Christ on their behalf have their faith strengthened by means of this sacrament, but it is a particularly potent means for those of a sacramental persuasion.

In any case, all these things provided for us as means of help will assist the Holy Spirit as He seeks to bring the life of Christ to reality within us.

Will the process ever be complete? Will it ever be true that Christ has gained access to every niche and corner of my heart and life? Unfortunately, no, it will never turn out that way. Despite what some popular Christian songs or speakers may say about total surrender or other verbiage of like ilk, not a one of us will ever be completely indwelt by Christ while we live on this planet. The old nature will always be with us as long as we live, so the work of the Holy Spirit will never be done, and we will never be completely Christ-filled or Christlike. Often we will find that we have stifled the work of the Holy Spirit while under the influence of the old nature, and sometimes we will even find that we have given up ground previously won with His help.

But praise be to God, His Holy Spirit will never give up on us; He will always remain at work within us urging us toward those things that will enable the life of Christ to gain ground in our hearts and lives and, in the process, we will become more like Him in our character and conduct. Indeed, the light that He brings into being within us will shine so clearly that men truly will see that our good deeds are a God-thing and give praise to our Father in heaven.

Into my heart, into my heart, come into my heart, Lord Jesus. We want you to be the light within us that we will shine out into the world within which you have placed us.

Chapter 4

What About Good Deeds?

What good is it, my brothers, if a man claims
to have faith but has no deeds? Can such faith
save him? Suppose a brother or sister is without
clothes and daily food. If one of you says to him,
"Go, I wish you well; keep warm and well fed,"
but does nothing about his physical needs, what
good is it? In the same say, faith by itself, if it
is not accompanied by action, is dead... As the
body without the spirit is dead, so faith without
deeds is dead.
James 2: 14-17, 26

On one occasion, after I had given a message on the topic of "Christ in me", one of our church leaders came up to me and basically said, "What you say is all well and good, but I know from personal experience that if I don't take the bull by the horns and make sure something gets done for Christ's kingdom, nothing will get done". While I can sympathize with that sentiment, I heartily disagree with such thinking. It epitomizes the bondage and "drivenness" I referred to at the outset of this work. Long experience has proven to me, and to many others like me, that when I "take the bull by the horns", I inevitably will eventually find out that, indeed, I do not have the bull by the horns, but, instead, the horns of the bull have got me. I expect you all have experienced that for yourselves all too often.

Trying to take matters completely into our own hands, in terms of living out our Christianity and getting things done for Christ's kingdom, will always lead to weariness and disillusionment. We were never meant to bear the brunt of that burden, as we discussed in the last chapter. Indeed, we are not capable of it. But as James so powerfully shows in the verses printed above, God most certainly does expect us to be involved in good deeds for the sake of His name and Christ's kingdom.

So, what gives?

Here in a nutshell is my account of how it works. Good deeds, for a Christian whose primary concern is to simply be what God intends him to be, are less individual actions than they are a lifestyle. As you live out the lifestyle outlined in chapter 3, availing yourself of the means of help provided for your use by the Holy Spirit, He will give you those urges and promptings that will release Christ within you to direct you to those activities and deeds that He (Christ) wants to accomplish through you. Christ Himself will enable and empower you, like He did my dad, to be the person He wants you to be to get what He wants to get done in a given situation or setting.

Will it always necessarily be stressless and smooth going? Of course not. The world, the devil, and the flesh of your own old nature will always be there to oppose what Christ is seeking to do through you. Sometimes it will be laborious and frustrating, but you will always be able to rest assured that the Christ dwelling in you is eminently capable of empowering and encouraging you, that He's the One who "takes the bull by the horns" and lives powerfully through you, and in the process shines from out of your life as a light that cannot be hidden.

Sometimes, this lifestyle is referred to in terms of being "Christ-like", and that is certainly in line with biblical truth, but, in our self-absorbed culture, the call to a lifestyle of Christlikeness too easily lends itself to becoming just another "to do" list, or worse yet, ending up simply as just another entry on an already existing and already too long "to do" list. That, simply put, is our American way of doing Christianity.

The WWJD (What Would Jesus Do) craze of a few years ago is a case in point. While its intent was good and meant to be Christ-honoring, it was a movement encouraging doing without any thought for an underlying being. The fact that, in isolation from the guidance and wisdom of the rest of Scripture, we were being encouraged to just get out there and do what Jesus would do, was in itself an implication that we need only to determine the correct course of action and then self reliantly and self sufficiently carry it out.

The Apostle Paul went down that route – perhaps on more than one occasion. He often spoke paradoxically of being at his strongest when he felt he was at his weakest. In 2 Corinthians 12, for example, he says: "I boast all the more gladly about my weaknesses, so that Christ's power may rest on me. That is why, for Christ's sake, I delight in weaknesses, in insults, in hardships, in persecutions, in difficulties. For when I am weak, then I am strong".

Truly, if we are living a lifestyle of repentance and faith in which we are led and prompted by the Spirit and empowered by the indwelling Christ, the good deeds that we are intended to be involved with will come to us as a matter of course, and we will find ourselves, and sometimes even be oblivious to the fact, that we are up to our eyebrows in Christ's kingdom work. We will find ourselves in the same boat as Peter and John who, when

41

told to refrain from working to advance Christ's kingdom said in Acts 4: "Judge for yourselves whether it is right in God's sight to obey you rather than God. For we cannot help speaking about what we have seen and heard".

When we are empowered and animated by Christ within us we will not have to worry about finding God's will for our lives. It will find us – and we will be led by the Spirit to enter into it without hesitation. The world, the Devil, and the old nature will attempt to hinder the work, but Christ WILL get his kingdom's work done through those of us whom He has called. If our relationship with Him is intact, like Peter and John, we will not be able to help ourselves from doing it.

We must always remember in this regard that the power referred to, the power to do good deeds for Christ and His kingdom, always and only comes from Christ Himself. Scripture is very clear on this. In John 15:5, Jesus says, "I am the vine; you are the branches. If a man remains in me and I in him, he will bear much fruit; apart

42

from me you can do nothing". The writer to the Hebrews says in Hebrews 13:20-21: "May the God of peace...equip you with everything good for doing his will, and may he work in us what is pleasing to him, through Jesus Christ...". And the Apostle Paul says very pointedly in Philippians 4:13: "I can do everything through him who gives me strength".

In my upbringing, I was taught to believe that our good deeds are done out of grateful response for all that God has done for me in Christ. I still subscribe to that view, but there is a danger even in this way of looking at it, for there is still the possibility of allowing too much "I-ness" into the picture - if we entertain the line of thinking that notes the fact that it is MY response and that there is some hint of heroism or self-empowerment in my having done so.

There is no thought of or room for heroism in the life of someone within whom and through whom Christ truly lives. The thought of heroism will likely only enter the

43

mind of such people when they receive unsolicited praise from other humans or when Satan is there to plant those seeds in order to knock them off course.

I don't believe that the ones we would include in the Christian Hall of Fame felt even a hint of heroism for what they did. They simply followed the urges and leading of the Holy Spirit, and with the empowerment of Christ within, they contentedly, matter-of-factly, did what we now consider to be great and awesome deeds done for the sake of the Lord and His kingdom. Often they probably did not know where all this would lead them, but that is really not much of an issue for one whose life is in tune with the triune God of the Bible.

It may also be, that in your life and mine, we may not know exactly where the desires of Christ within us will lead, but it is entirely possible to be completely contented with that state of affairs. Oswald Chambers refers to that state as "gracious uncertainty" and in his book, "The Love of God", he says: "Certainty is the mark of the common-sense life; gracious uncertainty is the mark of the spiritual life, and they must both go together. Mathematics is the rule of reason and common sense, but faith and hope is the rule of the spiritual. 'What we will be has not yet appeared' (I John 3:2) – we are gloriously uncertain of the next step, but we are certain of God. Immediately we abandon to God and do the duty that lies nearest, he packs our lives with surprises all the time..."[2]

The Apostle Paul once said: "For God, who said, 'Let light shine out of darkness,' made His light shine in our hearts to give us the light of the knowledge of the glory of God in the face of Christ. But, we have this treasure in jars of clay to show that this all-surpassing power is from God and not from us. We are hard pressed on every side, but not crushed; perplexed, but not in despair; persecuted, but not abandoned; struck down, but not destroyed. We always carry around in our body the death of Jesus, so that the life of Jesus may also be revealed in our body. For we who are alive are always being given over to death for

Jesus' sake, so that His life may be revealed in our mortal body" (2 Corinthians 4:6-11). Christ's life will be revealed in the lives of Christians who embrace His gift of "gracious uncertainty", but He is the one who will power the process through us, His jars of clay. We are indeed privileged to be called to be one of those jars, and if we truly allow Christ to make of us a jar of his design, then pure and unadulterated joy will be ours.

Chapter 5

Parting Shots: Why Not Enjoy Life With Christ?

[Jesus says:] You are already clean because of the
word I have spoken to you. Remain in me and
I will remain in you. No branch can bear fruit
by itself; it must remain in the vine. Neither can
you bear fruit unless you remain in me. I am the
vine; you are the branches. If a man remains in
me and I in him, he will bear much fruit; apart
from me you can do nothing.
(John 15:3-5)

At this point, it is logical to ask: If having Christ
living in me and through me can be so liberating and satisfying, why do there seem to be so few
Christians actually experiencing that kind of joyful existence? Why is there so little fruit, and why is so much of

the fruit I do see in Christians bittersweet at best? That is the same question I laid out for our consideration right at the outset of this writing. Why indeed?

The fault certainly does not lie with Christ. The Scripture passages we have brought forward so far bear witness to the fact that He greatly desires to live within us in an ever deepening relationship. In His own words: "I have come that they may have life and have it to the full" (John 10:10). So it is us who are throwing the wrench into the works. But why?

There are probably several reasons for it. We don't seem to have any problems with the idea of Christ living in our hearts and lives when we first receive Him into our lives. We are overjoyed that He would even consider doing so. But as we get a few miles down the road in our walk with Him, we tend to become a little tenuous, even skittish, about this whole idea of Christ in me. The initial excitement of having Him there is gone and now we aren't so sure we really want Him there, or at least

48

to what extent we want Him there. It can seem crowded and confining; we feel like we need to be doing things on our own. Should we really be relying so much on the fact that Christ lives in me? Sometimes it makes us feel uncomfortable.

People have always felt a little uncomfortable with the idea of Christ in me. We know what happened in John 6, when Jesus first delivered his "I am the bread of life" message and said things like, "Whoever eats my flesh and drinks my blood has eternal life, and I will raise him up at the last day. For my flesh is real food and my blood is real drink. Whoever eats my flesh and drinks my blood remains in me, and I in him" (vv 54-56). People got uncomfortable with this idea and verse 66 tells us that "from this time many of his disciples turned back and no longer followed him". It was threatening to them even then, way back at the beginning. And nothing has changed since then.

49

Some people may experience a theological discomfort when presented with the concept of Christ in me. How can Christ be in the lives of millions of Christians and still be at the right hand of God the Father interceding for us, as Scripture makes clear He does?. And how can both God the Holy Spirit and God the Son both be living and working within us at the same time? Is there really room for both of them in there?

These issues are easily answered. If you truly believe that Jesus is God then He is omnipresent, ubiquitous if you please, and being in the lives of millions of believers while sitting at the right hand of God the Father is not a problem in the least. And as for having both God the Holy Spirit and God the Son working in you simultaneously, remember what Paul says in Ephesians 3:16-17: "I pray that out of his glorious riches he may strengthen you with power through his Spirit in your inner being, so that Christ may dwell in your hearts through faith". Notice that reference is made to the Spirit in your inner being, but also to Christ dwelling in you. (And passages like 2 John 9 make it clear that God the Father is there as well.) If you are letting such issues stop you from accepting the concept of "Christ in me", then you are simply letting the god of your own reason have precedence over the God of the Bible and the basic tenets of our Christian faith. You yourself must deal with that issue before you can hope to move on in your faith.

While some are bothered by theological issues, I believe the grand majority of people who are uncomfortable with the idea of Christ living in them are that way primarily because of egotism and/or self-protecting psychologies. Here are three ways this may exhibit itself in us:

1. We want to be self-reliant and do things ourselves in our own way. We are prideful and self-sufficient. After all, we have been taught

by American culture that this is admirable
and right.

2. We are afraid of what cultivating the inner life
might really mean for us. It seems like it might
lead us into territory that could end up being
very humiliating, very revealing, maybe even
life-changing. The sad truth often is that we
would rather keep everything about us and
around us just the way it is.

3. We are uncomfortable with the uncertainty of
where "Christ in me" may lead and of what
He might have in mind for me. We want to
maintain control of the future.

Let me address each of these lines of thinking in turn:

First, why would you want to continue to hang on
to the futile idea that you can be self-reliant spiritually
and pull yourself up by your own spiritual bootstraps?
Haven't you already experienced that spiritual self-reli-

ance and relying on a lot of your own "doing" leaves you cold and disheartened? Only with Christ living in you and working with you can you truly experience the joy and liberty of, first, being what He intends you to be, and then simply allowing Him to lead and empower you in the life of service He has graciously planned for you.

Second, you must ask yourself, "What do I really treasure"? Is it the externalities of the things of this earth, the apparent security of a temporal status quo? Or is it the things of heaven, that inner life with Christ that can enable you to see that which really is important, that which has value and significance that will stretch on into eternity? One thing is certain; you can't have it both ways.

Third, as unlikely and unreasonable as it may seem, "gracious uncertainty" is a liberating way of life and a gift from God. Go back and read the section on that subject in chapter four of this book. Life with Christ in you and working in you in new and wonderful, albeit unforeseeable ways, is, in the long run, the only way to experience a contented, even relaxed, Christian existence.

Christ in me. It is a wonderful life; in fact, it's the only wonderful life there is to be had. It may not be comfortable all the time, it may not be an easy lifestyle, but it is truly chock full of joy, because with Christ, the God of the universe and Savior of the world living in me, nothing else seems nearly so important. And as the Holy Spirit continues working hard within me as well, to gain even more access to my life for Christ to occupy, the future only looks better.

One of the pastors in my past life used to greet the children of the congregation by placing his hand on their heads and saying, "Jesus Christ loves you and lives within you". How often in my adult years have I wanted and needed to go back and hear and internalize that simple declaration. The desire to be a person within whom the living Christ dwells is truly the deepest need and desire of every human heart.

Do you have that desire? Do you want to enjoy life with Christ? Do you want to reclaim the joyful essence of your Christianity? Then abide in Christ, and He will abide in you. Fix your eyes on Jesus. Focus less on doing and more on simply being the person Christ intends for you to be, a person through whom He Himself will live. Allow the Holy Spirit to use God's Word, self examination, confession, and all the other spiritual tools and means of help available for your use as He gently guides your focus constantly back to Jesus. As this happens, you will find joy and freedom flowing back into your Christian experience, and, rest assured, the doing part will certainly follow, not as an odious duty, but as a natural part of being a person motivated, enabled, and empowered by the living Christ within you.

Abide in Christ, and He will abide in you.

Notes

1. Charles Stanley, quoted from the March 30, 2011 broadcast of "In Touch".

2. Oswald Chambers, *The Love Of God,* quoted in *The Oswald Chambers Devotional Bible* (Wheaton, Ill.: Crossway Books, 2009).

Appendix

Selected Scripture Passages Dealing With Christ In Me

1. John 6:48-56

2. John 15:4-5

3. John 17:22-26

4. Romans 8:9-11

5. Romans 15:18

6. 2 Corinthians 13:5-6

7. Galatians 2:20

8. Galatians 4:19-20

9. Ephesians 3:16-17a

10. Colossians 1:26-27

11. Colossians 3:3-4

12. Colossians 3:9-11

13. Hebrews 13:20-21

14. I John 3:23-24

15. I John 4:4

16. I John 5:12,20

17. 2 John 9

18. Revelation 3:19-20

CPSIA information can be obtained at www.ICGtesting.com
Printed in the USA
BVOW08s1053180214

345274BV00001B/3/P